COLOR ME *green*

Color Me Green is published by
Business Publications Corporation Inc., an Iowa corporation.

Copyright © 2018 by Pat Brown.

Reproduction or other use, in whole or in part, of the contents
without permission of the publisher is strictly prohibited.

ISBN: 9780996721376
Library of Congress Control Number: 2018946522
Business Publications Corporation Inc., Des Moines, IA

bpc

Business Publications Corporation Inc.
The Depot at Fourth
100 4th Street
Des Moines, Iowa 50309
(515) 288-3336

color me green

me

written by PAT BROWN   illustrations by JOHANNA PIEPEL

This book is dedicated to Max and Amy Hawkins, my grandchildren.
May they color their future green.

Color Me Green

I wrote this book because I found so many women who were intimidated by finances and didn't know where to get an understanding about insurance, credit cards and credit scores. I know some women who won't answer the phone or open mail because a collection agency has sent the letter or is on the phone. Other women live paycheck to paycheck because they haven't learned some basic concepts of handling money and making the right financial decision. They think it's better to ignore the problem. However, the debt and stress don't go away.

Where to begin? Start simple; don't try to build a clock when you haven't learned how to tell time. Why bother? Wouldn't you like to save money when buying that new car, or even better, borrow money for a new home? The following pages teach some basic concepts and provide a foundation to build your financial knowledge. So start coloring your way to being financially savvy.

Start simple; don't try to build a clock when you haven't learned how to tell time.

Credit Scores

Understanding finances seems overwhelming to Judy, who just started her first serious job as the manager at a big-box store. She will be the first to admit that she doesn't understand very much about credit scores, loans, credit cards — in short, most financial transactions. And she doesn't know where to learn how to become financially savvy.

If I were acting as Judy's financial coach, my first question to her would be this: "What do you think is your most valuable asset?"

Judy rents, so she would probably say it's her new car. If Judy owned a home, she might answer her home. While both things have value, the real valuable asset is her credit score and earning power.

Let's discuss credit score, and what Judy needs to understand about credit scores and why they are important. When Judy has credit and an acceptable credit score, she has financial power.

While credit bureaus like Equifax, Experian and more report credit transactions, the company Fair Isaac Corp., abbreviated as FICO, tracks Judy's use of credit cards, loans and other debts — this includes whether Judy pays her bills on time — to create a FICO score or credit score.

Judy needs to know what her credit score is and how it is calculated. Lenders look at separate components, not just the total score, in assessing the risk of lending her money.

Credit score numbers range from 350 to 850 and are based on these standards:

1. Judy needs to pay her bills when due. Payment history is 35% of her score.

2. How much debt Judy carries will also affect her credit score. If she borrows the maximum amount of her available credit, she will negatively affect her credit score. For example, if Judy has a $2,000 limit on her credit card but doesn't carry over more than $200, or 10% of her limit, the loan officer will think Judy spends wisely. Judy will need to reduce her debt to 10% or less of her credit limit. The amount of money Judy borrows relative to her available credit accounts for 30% of her score.

3. Building a good credit score takes time because the longer Judy has borrowed money successfully, the better her score will be. Judy should keep old credit cards open even if she isn't charging on them anymore. The length of time you have borrowed money accounts for 15% of your credit score.

4. The kind of debt you have also counts. If all your debt is in credit cards, you will get a 10% negative score. If you have a responsible mix of student loans, car payments and low credit card debt, you will have a better outlook.

5. Be cautious about signing up for new credit cards. Retailers will tempt Judy with discounts if she signs up for their credit card. Ten % of Judy's score will be based on her applying for a new credit card, and lenders will need to check her credit score in order to see if she is a good risk. Any entity checking your credit score has a negative impact on the score and can lower it. Lots of new cards and credit checks in a short period of time will have a negative effect on the score.

Where can you find your credit score and credit history? Congress passed the Fair Credit Reporting Act, which gave citizens have the right to access their credit history.

You have one free access annually. While some credit card companies and banks regularly inform their customers of their credit score, they do not provide details about the transactions.

Lenders will assess Judy's ability to pay back a loan and take into account her occupation, salary and length of employment along with her credit score.

To obtain a copy of your report, contact any of the three national credit bureaus:

Equifax: P.O. Box 105873, Atlanta, GA 30348; 800-685-1111; www.equifax.com

Experian: P.O. Box 2104, Allen, TX 75013-2104; www.experian.com

TransUnion: P.O. Box 390, Springfield, PA 19064-0390; 800-888-4213; transunion.com

...the real valuable asset is her credit score and earning power

Credit Cards & Credit Card Debt

Skip this chapter if you don't carry a credit card balance from month to month and you create a budget, follow it and pay the balance on your credit card every month. However, Judy maxed out her credit cards because she didn't understand how to use a credit card and the consequences of credit card debt.

Judy felt so overwhelmed by her credit card debt and other bills, she wouldn't open her mail. She avoided answering the phone, cried a lot and couldn't sleep. She lived from paycheck to paycheck. Judy is an extreme case and probably needs a financial counselor.

Getting out of credit card debt requires a commitment. Like losing weight sensibly, eliminating credit card debt requires a plan. The plan begins with finding out where you are and what resources you have and setting up goals you can successfully achieve. It helps to ask a friend to be your support and partner in this process. Judy has spent more than she earns, and that got her into financial trouble. Not knowing what she owes and being afraid to find out and continuing to spend money without a plan will keep her in a financial quagmire.

Judy may have to use a debit card for purchases and commit to paying the total amount owed on her credit card bill every month. If she is unable to follow her commitment, her best remedy would be to cut up all credit cards. Her first step in gaining control of her finances is knowing where she spends her money and awareness of the consequences of making only the minimum monthly payments on her credit card.

Budgeting

Judy purchased a small notebook and started writing down everything she spent. She planned to do this for one month. She recorded the morning latte bought at the coffee shop, the new music download she just had to have. She included the must-pay bills such as rent, utilities and her car payment. On a separate page she wrote down all the bills she owed but hadn't paid. This exercise made Judy aware of how she spent her paycheck and what she owed. After one month of monitoring her spending habits, she organized her list into categories: must-pay bills such as rent, utilities, etc. Then she constructed her impulsive buying list and her food list from ordering a fast-food lunch every day. Critical to this exercise is knowing how you spend money buying groceries. Everyone's list will be as different as the people who create the list.

This exercise made Judy aware of how she spent her paycheck and what she owed.

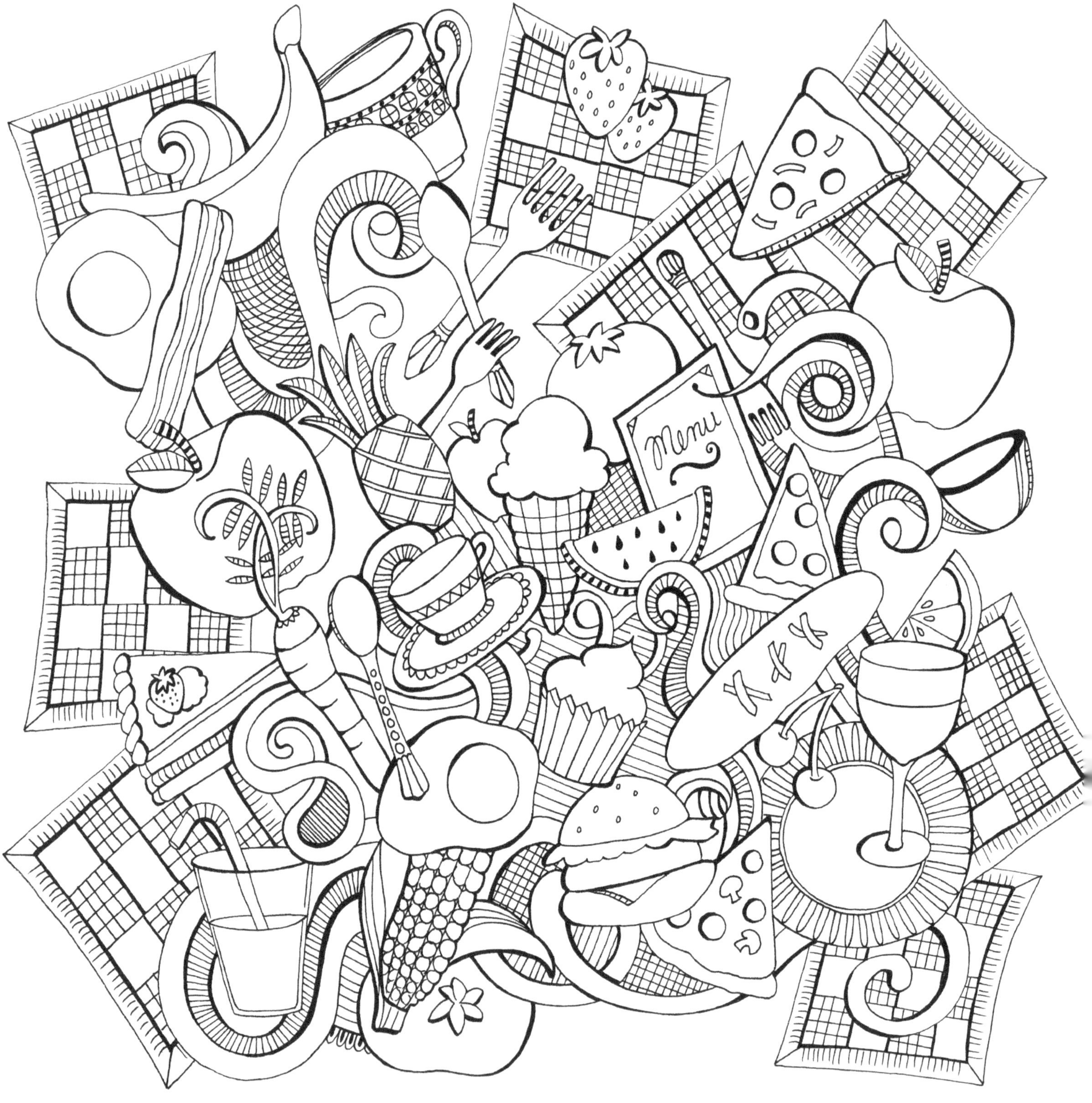
Menu

Judy realized that she ate lunch at fast-food restaurants. With a five-day workweek, she was spending $5 to $6 a day on lunch. She decided to make a lunch and planned her grocery list so that she spent one-half of the daily cost of the fast-food lunch on her made-at-home lunch.

To recap, Judy had a few issues that put her in trouble:

1. Lack of a plan.

2. Lack of patience.

3. Failure to document personal business records like balancing her checkbook.

To remedy this, Judy became fiscally responsible by:

1. Making a decision to eliminate her credit card debt.

2. Creating a plan with specific steps like bring a sack lunch to work instead of eating out.

3. Partnering with a friend for support and accountability.

4. Rewarding herself with a treat, whether it be eating lunch out or buying a latte at the coffee shop.

Renter's Insurance

Judy just signed a lease for her first apartment. She bought some furniture and furnished her kitchen with cookware and dishes. She also bought a bed and dresser and brought her television and laptop from home. She thinks her landlord will cover her personal property if there was a fire in the apartment complex.

If her personal property is destroyed in a fire, Judy will discover that the landlord not only does not cover her personal property, the landlord is not required to find or pay for alternate housing. Worse, if Judy's candle started the fire, the landlord could sue her for the damage caused by her candle starting an apartment fire.

Imagine this scenario:

Judy invited friends over for dinner and was frying chicken on the stove. Her cellphone, located in her bedroom, rang and she left the kitchen to answer the phone. Hot grease splattered out of the pan and started a fire. By the time the smoke alarms went off and Judy ran to the kitchen, her window curtains were aflame. She ran out of the apartment, alerting neighbors on the way out.

Judy will discover that the landlord not only does not cover her personal property, the landlord is not required to find or pay for alternate housing.

*Renter's insurance is one of the most
affordable products on the insurance market.*

Judy had neglected to buy renter's insurance. Her personal property loss amounted to $20,000. She moved in with a friend and used her credit card to replace clothes so that she could show up at work the next day dressed professionally. She fretted about her landlord suing her. Even though the fire department reacted promptly and only her apartment had damage, the other apartments were not habitable because of smoke damage.

Renter's insurance is one of the most affordable products on the insurance market. Judy can afford a pizza every month when she and her friends go out, and for the price of a pizza, she can afford renter's insurance.

Exactly what does renter's insurance protect? Most policies cover damage from fire, lightning, any kind of wind such as tornado or hurricane, hail, explosion, riot, aircraft and automobiles colliding with the building, smoke, vandalism, theft, and weight of ice, snow or sleet, just to name a few of the protected losses. Always read your policy carefully to see what losses are covered under the policy and what losses are excluded. Some items such as jewelry have special limits. Ask about special limits on some types of personal property.

Documenting what you own, an inventory, will help with a claim. Especially important are those serial numbers on electronics. Photograph your stuff and store the photos in the cloud or anywhere off the premises.

Check to see if your policy replaces the lost item with "like quality." Replacement cost means that the company pays for a replacement item of like quality. This is where the inventory is important, especially the photos and serial numbers. You provide documentation of what you owned so that the insurance company can evaluate the appropriate replacement item. If you choose to forgo replacing the item, the company will pay actual cash value. If you paid $300 for a table and that same quality of table now costs $400, the company will pay for a $400 replacement. If, however, you choose not to replace the table and you choose to take a cash settlement, the company will start with the $400 and, using depreciation charts, subtract for wear and tear. Some items cannot be replaced, such as antiques, paintings, etc. You need to ask how your particular company handles these kinds of claims.

All renter's policies have a deductible on personal property losses. There is no deductible for liability losses. For example, if you lose $10,000 of property in a fire, and you carry $500 deductible, you would pay for the first $500 of the total loss.

Judy needs to choose a policy with inflation coverage. The policy amount is increased annually by an inflation index such as the consumer price index. If Judy has inflation protection, she will be able to replace her property at current prices.

Finally Judy needs to protect herself by making sure her landlord has installed smoke and carbon monoxide detectors. Test the devices every month. Deadbolt locks are the best protection against theft. Lock your door even when you are in the apartment. Never leave the apartment with an unlocked door. Judy needs to make sure her landlord has the heating and cooling devices inspected annually. Have an escape plan.

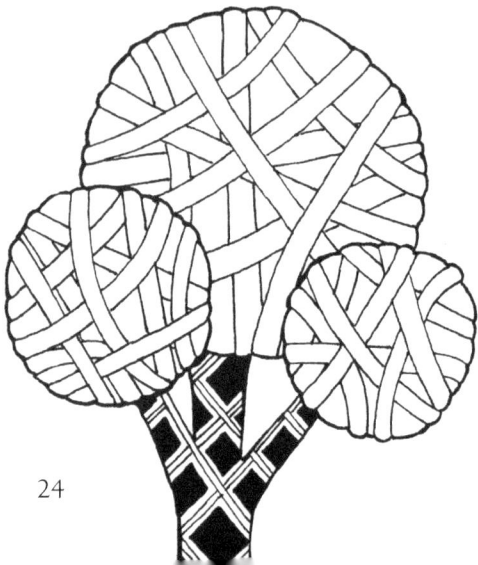

Summary

Are you ready to own your financial tomorrow? You've read and colored the book, but now what?

Financial knowledge is power, but the knowledge of financial fundamentals is just the first step. Build another stair by choosing just one thing you are going to change.

Here are a few suggestions: Buy a renter's policy to protect your stuff. Make a plan to pay off your credit card. Make your lunch at home instead of buying fast food to save enough to pay off a debt.

There are any number of websites to help you learn more. Your bank or insurance company probably has financial education on their website as well as calculators to calculate monthly installments using varying interest rates that show you how much you save if you qualify for a lower interest rate.

Taking responsibility for your financial decisions is about more than money. Taking control of your financial decisions builds confidence and self-esteem.

You never know — by building financial knowledge and committing to change one step at a time, you might wind up with a staircase and a fat savings account.

www.ingramcontent.com/pod-product-compliance
Lightning Source LLC
Chambersburg PA
CBHW052045190326
41520CB00002BA/198